Surviving Learning
Disabilities Successfully

Surviving Learning Disabilities Successfully

◆

16 Rules for Managing a Child's Learning Disabilities

A Remarkable True Story

Nancy E. Graves
Danielle E. Graves

iUniverse, Inc.
New York Lincoln Shanghai

Surviving Learning Disabilities Successfully
16 Rules for Managing a Child's Learning Disabilities

iUniverse books may be ordered through booksellers or by contacting:

iUniverse
2021 Pine Lake Road, Suite 100
Lincoln, NE 68512
www.iuniverse.com
1-800-Authors (1-800-288-4677)

Because of the dynamic nature of the Internet, any Web addresses or links contained in this book may have changed since publication and may no longer be valid.

The views expressed in this work are solely those of the author and do not necessarily reflect the views of the publisher, and the publisher hereby disclaims any responsibility for them.

ISBN: 978-0-595-45637-6 (pbk)
ISBN: 978-0-595-89940-1 (ebk)

Printed in the United States of America

Dedicated with our love to Phyllis A. Graves, Burt Graves and Megan Marrin Graves

We want to express our love and gratitude to our family who has been a constant source of love and support throughout our journey. Special thanks to: teacher Susan King who was our light, learning consultant Marie Ferzacca our steadfast fan, Karen McConnell who is always in our corner, and Ted May of University of Denver, who saw us through the DU finish line. And to Alan, for the love we share which completes our family.

Contents

Foreword: From Nancy

Her chocolate eyes are so dark that from the moment she was born it was like a magical image, at times I would see into her eyes and at other times I would see my reflection. Our connection to our child, the person she is and the person we want to be for her, is what guides us through uncharted territory and brings us through victorious. This is a story of a fight waged for my child and one that was won by her.

My daughter Danielle, was diagnosed with profound learning disabilities when she was four years old. The prognosis from the cast of professionals was so bleak that it was suggested a 'special school' might yield the only hope of a modified education, if she could learn at all. They told me she would most likely never learn to read or write.

Nothing prepares us for such staggering news. How can a child who looks, acts and feels perfectly healthy, have a disability that will affect her entire life?

I listened to the many experts at that conference table in 1988, walked out into the wet, dark winter night and sat in my car stunned while tears fell onto my jacket. How could this darling, infectious, beautiful child be so limited? How could her life be forecast with such certainty? I, like most, have faced my share of harrowing times, but that night in the car, the drone of traffic on Highway 40 and sheets of rain all around, still stands as one of the darkest days of my life.

Give me any challenge and I will face it, but this was a life size challenge my child would live with and one I could not control. With my daughters waiting at home with a babysitter, I knew my time was limited. Mine was not a life that allowed for meltdowns. I gripped the steering wheel and headed for home. I didn't know the plan, but I knew the outcome; I would do whatever it took to provide a limitless future for Danielle. It was the promise I gave both of my daughters from birth and a roundtable of psychologists and educators could not take that away.

When I opened the front door Megan, my nine year old daughter, leaned into me with her arm reaching around me to hold my waist. Her head pressed into my hip, holding on tight, as we awaited the inevitable crash as Danielle ran forward and clutched my leg. She held on with both arms with her face turned up to me. That face was as open and alive as always. While I was numb with pain and sadness we stood holding on to one another laughing, talking all at once and hobbling along (none of us willing to let go) to the kitchen to try the cookies they had baked. Not a word was said that might indicate that they sensed my upset, but they protected me with their little bodies and I refueled during the crumbs and the milk spills. I wandered the house all night watching the girls sleeping, searching and finding the seed of hope within me.

For the next eighteen years that hope would be beaten, shattered, ridiculed and at moments lost, but it triumphed along with Danielle. We learned together that while you can become battle weary on the hills along the way, you must live to fight another day or you will never make it to the mountain. Danielle is about her dreams with no limits. Danielle didn't know what the experts said when she was four and when she was old enough to understand she didn't care. The many voices who would tell her she couldn't achieve and wouldn't have a normal life were silenced by our voices. Danielle's mountain is every dream she may ever have and that is where we set our sites.

This journey sometimes felt bigger than both of us, but we traveled with determination and guts. Far too often when Danielle accomplished something the experts had told us she would never be able to do, they would then say that we should settle, be satisfied. But every time we reached a milestone, we looked for the next and the next. While there were many voices telling me that she had accomplished more than she was ever expected to achieve, we were still unwilling to settle. Danielle didn't know the extent of her so-called limitations and I didn't accept them.

This book chronicles some of our journey. We share this most personal struggle because we know how tough it is. Perhaps you will find hope and inspiration in our story. Perhaps we can provide you with some practical tools and the fuel to get you energized for the fights of your life. The battles we fight for our children are torn from our hearts. If we are to persevere there must be nothing to deter us, nothing to defeat us. Look into your child's eyes and know that only you can fight for the person you see there. There are many hills between now and that mountain, but they are strategic battles you can plan for and win. The mountain is the future you promised your child with his or her first breath.

Danielle's academic battles aren't over, she plans to attend graduate school, but she is on the mountain now. Danielle arrived on the mountain when she graduated from college in June, 2006. It is a place we were told she would never be. She has fought the stigmas, the stereotypes and the ignorance by living her life fully. There was a time when she said she couldn't wait to get as far away from learning disabilities as possible. Now she has chosen to devote her life to children and families who are facing the same challenges she faced. And who better to ease this difficult road?

Danielle is one of the most remarkable people I have ever known. She has inspired teachers throughout her education. She has reminded some why they became teachers and sparked a passion in others to fight the fight with us. And she has touched many, many lives. My love, respect and admiration for her are immeasurable. She continues to climb the mountain but now she has an unfair advantage. She is stronger and tougher than most young people because of all she has faced and conquered.

Being told that your child has learning disabilities brings denial, fear, sadness, frustration and determination. You will need a plan, a timeline and the capacity to learn what is behind the eyes of your child. You will also need your sense of humor, your sense of the ridiculous and a stomach for the absurd. Your child has only one chance to receive an education without which she can't achieve her dreams. We will share with you how to survive the battles and how to live to reach the mountain.... because if you die on the hill, you won't make it to the mountain!

Foreword:
From Danielle

My Mom and I worked together to write this book as we have always worked together … tirelessly and openly. We decided the story would best be written in her voice. For clarity we use *she* throughout our story rather than *he/she*.

I can't think about our journey without feelings of absolute and profound love and respect for my Mom. When I was in high school we had an assignment to write about our hero. Many kids wrote about famous people in history. I wrote about my Mom. She is a beautiful, open face with a huge heart and smile. Her touch is gentle and rock solid. Her laughter is quick, her patience enormous and her ability to listen draws people like a magnet. We can laugh together, cook together and be alone together. She makes everywhere a home by her ability to soften the outside world and make us feel safe inside.

My Mom is my hero because she represents all that is life to me. She isn't perfect and she isn't afraid to admit it. I believe I can do anything because she says it and she lives it. I have personal values we share that guide me. If I can remain strong, self confident and kind then I will live up to what she dreams for me. And I will live a life willing to give to others. My Mom is a daily example of what is possible.

As you read our story I hope that you whether as a parent, teacher, grandparent, friend or student will be inspired to be a hero to a child.

Rule # 1: Trust No One

Once your child is evaluated by professionals you may think there are experts on the case. Not so. Something brought you to the professional's den. Perhaps you noticed something about your child that didn't sit right with you and you sought a professional's opinion. Maybe the school alerted you to concerns about particular skills or learning milestones that they felt were not within the norms (ah, a word we come to hate). Experts in the learning field possess opinions only, not gospel. Seek many and keep few.

Most of us are expert at what we do. My initial reaction was to respect the apparent fact that the people I was dealing with were:

a. experts,

b. devoted to children,

c. knew more than I did,

d. should be trusted,

e. understood the system,

f. would have answers.

All wrong. Assume the exact opposite at all times. While this may seem a cynical statement, it is advice you will credit with many of the best decisions you will make.

When you submit your child for testing that is an admission that there may be a problem. When psychologists, psychiatrists and state education officials seat themselves at a big table and zero in on you, they are doing what they do for a living. Some are more experienced and educated than others. Some don't know what they're doing. Others had a fight with their spouse that morning and aren't even in the meeting. But, because this is all new, and it is your child you naturally will see them as the experts and yourself as the novice. In reality, everyone in the room is a novice when it comes to your child. Why? Because your child is unique. And when you walk out of that room with a label for your child, learning disabled, language impaired, you must manage that diagnosis as a tool—not as a definition of your child.

When I left the initial evaluation for Danielle I was overwhelmed. They explained that she had multiple and profound learning disabilities. She would need to go to a special school and most likely would never learn to read or write. One psychiatrist even offered her forty years of experience on a *subjective note* that she believed my divorce had exacerbated Danielle's situation. Since I was ripe for more guilt, I asked if it was something I had done, perhaps eaten the wrong foods when I was pregnant or read <u>Goodnight Moon</u> above the recommended one hundred times. There was a lot of head shaking from the experts, but no rush to let me off the hook. By the time I got home and had Danielle on my lap telling me all about her day I knew I had to do two things: get a second opinion and find the right elementary school for her.

Rule # 2: No Time for Denial

My experience is that mistakes are made all of the time. But, if you receive the results of a battery of tests and receive a diagnosis, then you must accept that there is something going on that you need to deal with on behalf of your child. This is not the time for denial. We all say to ourselves it can't be true about our child. We may mangle, if not kill the messenger. But, after we act out, as we must, it is time for a second opinion. Whether the first evaluation was done by the public school department or through a private source you should take your test results and get a second opinion.

I made appointments with every learning expert in town. That was just my starting point as I would have expanded the resource reach if I didn't find what I wanted. At every appointment I carried Danielle's file. But three of the first four people never saw her file. I began each meeting by giving them a picture of Danielle. I wanted them to see that she was not a stack of standardized tests but a vibrant four year old child. The first three learning consultants gave the picture a cursory look and began explaining the perils of the learning disabled. I spent less than thirty minutes with each of them. The fourth person held Danielle's photo and asked what she was like. What she liked to do and what made her laugh. He was captivated by her face and he sought her individuality. He agreed to read the file but not until he could meet Danielle in person and get to know her a little. I brought Danielle back the next day and she spent an hour with him. He spoke to me with Danielle seated right next to me. He told us that Danielle was a bright and curious person and that she had so much to do in her life. He spoke about her with such positive and limitless thoughts. I left there taking the first deep breath in the six weeks since the first evaluation meeting.

In the days to follow he studied her test results, ran a few additional tests and gave me some great direction. He said she didn't need a special school; she needed to be in regular school. But she would thrive in a structured classroom. He also said that there should be no more talk of holding her back a year as was suggested by some experts. This so called 'gift of time' was only going to rob her of the ability to interact with children her own age and, while she needed to learn in her own way, time was not an antidote for learning differently.

We visited the three public schools in the best district in our area. We visited every private school. The private schools made it clear that they could not and would not accommodate (another word you come to hate) her learning disabilities. While public schools are required by law to do so, private schools are not and they had no interest in making an exception. That was actually a good thing because my tendency was to believe that a private school was a better education opportunity than public school but, for us, that was not the case. We found the school we thought was best for Danielle and did another very tough thing, we moved into the school district. Leaving the home we loved was inexplicable to my very sad daughters, but I shut the door that housed all of their childhood memories with a clear understanding of why I had to do so. Mine were the only dry eyes as we drove away for the last time.

Rule # 3: Believe No One

My work experience has taught me to seek the best minds on a particular problem or subject and to value their opinion. This does not extend to my personal life where a more cynical stance exists. The challenge was to combine my professional and personal processes into a more beneficial approach for tackling the school bureaucracy. From Danielle's first day of elementary school right through her last college course the following phrases became a familiar refrain from teachers and administrators: can't do it, won't do it, and don't have to do it. There may be a reluctance to argue with people who are experts in education but you'll need to get over that.

Instead of starting with an attitude of believe everything they say until it is proven wrong, you should believe no one and believe nothing. Why? Because they are protecting their limited resources and their rules. That inherently puts you and the school at cross purposes and does not automatically provide what is best to meet your child's needs. You are the only person who can act on behalf of your child. The school district's financial and/or attitudinal constraints are not your problem. You have entered an inherently adversarial relationship between your child and the educators.

Federal law protects children with diagnosed learning disabilities. If you aren't familiar with what they are you need to obtain a copy of the guidelines and understand what they mean. The bottom line is that your child, once diagnosed with a learning disability, is protected under federal law and entitled to receive an education and to do so in the least restrictive environment. You need to be fully informed about the laws protecting your child and your child's documented accommodations contained in their Individual Education Plan (IEP).

While being protected by law sounds good it is always a battle for the limited resources of the school district. What does this mean? The Individuals with Disabilities Education Act (IDEA) was originally created by the government in 1975. It has been updated in 1990 and in 2004. The update in 2004, with final guidelines released in August, 2006 expands the responsibilities of the school districts. Virtually without exception, parents will still need to fight for the educational resources for their child.

In order to be covered by IDEA, prior to the most recent revisions, your child needed to be tested and documented to have a learning disability. This diagnosis carried with it specific education requirements that the school district was compelled to comply with. That has not changed. However, there are new guidelines that will include more children than ever under the IDEA umbrella.

As part of the No Child Left Behind initiative, the new guidelines are intended to identify children who are not performing at the class standard as early as first or second grade and intervene in very specific ways to support them to close the gap. The three levels of defined intervention intensify over a period of time in an effort to address deficiencies.

Some experts believe that this new set of guidelines for early intervention will most likely address environmental deficits for children and probably not identify highly intelligent, gifted children who aren't performing up to their potential due to learning disabilities. One reality has to be that there will be more pressure than ever on the school districts to meet the expanded legal requirements of IDEA. As a parent you will still have to fight to get the resources for your child. Know your child's rights under the law and be prepared to elevate the discussion with school administrators.

As you come to grips with the realities of your child's school and your state's funding, you will need to become the face and the voice for your child. There is a media and public relations tactic that we can employ in the education arena. When people are interviewed and asked questions they generally have prepared statements or messages that they will repeat over and over no matter what the question. When a celebrity is asked about his newborn baby he'll say, "She's great and I can't wait to see her after the launch of my new movie.... ." When asked if the baby will be making a public appearance soon, he replies, "This movie was everything we hoped for and you won't be disappointed." You get the idea.

So, what are your messages?

• How is my child doing?

- Can you be specific?

- May I see some of her work?

- What is she working on?

- How does her time as defined by the IEP compare with the actual resource being provided?

- May I see the classroom schedules?

You want to become a familiar face to everyone who interacts with your child.

You are interested in exactly what is being implemented in the school setting to help your child learn. You are interested in exactly what progress she is making.

Stop by the classroom several times a week. Be a room parent. Volunteer at every possible opportunity. Stop the counselor in the hall. Be known to the principal and every member of the office staff. And make those visits as positive as possible because you may be perceived as a negative presence before you know it.

You are interested in obtaining information. When a teacher says your child is doing fine, you need to ask, "Can you be more specific?" Your child is such a joy to have in class. "Really, in what way?" You need to ask to see your child's school work <u>before</u> parent's night. Ask for a portfolio of work so that you can actually see what they are doing at school. When children are in first through at least third or fourth grade there may be little in a backpack to provide clues for what is happening at school. Don't believe that 'no news is good news.' Get the facts early and take action.

Believing no one may sound overly cynical, but it isn't. Teachers are well intentioned but often young and inexperienced. Or, they may be protected by tenure (enough said). The majority are good but they have too many students and not enough help. And, almost without exception, they are completely under educated and under trained regarding learning disabilities. That fact, combined with limited resources, makes you the only person who will fight for what your child needs. When you are told the classroom of twenty five doesn't allow for your child to get the one-on-one accommodation she needs, don't accept it. If you are advised that the Individual Education Plan (IEP) is being followed and you still have concerns, ask for a meeting. When the school contacts you for an IEP meeting get it on your schedule, prepare lists of your concerns and questions, and be sure there is adequate time for you to listen to their reports and address your list as well.

The report from school that your child is doing fine is not something that should give you comfort. In fact, a child with learning disabilities in an average size classroom who, according to the teacher, is doing fine may actually be falling through the cracks. You may not hear the giant sucking noise as they are swallowed up, but they are sinking. Why? If they have a learning disability and no behavioral problems that may be disruptive or noticeable to the classroom teacher, they may appear to be the ideal student. They sit in silence and don't demand attention. Of course, they appear to be fine and they are a respite for the teacher, but they aren't receiving what they need to learn. That is where you come in.

When Danielle was in the first grade I went to visit her classroom in the third week of school. The room was decorated and so inviting. The children were all so animated and cute. I sat in the back of the classroom until the bell rang and children were directed to put their things in their desks and go to recess. I walked up to Danielle who was still standing by her desk. Her face lit up as she reached for my hand. The teacher walked over and told me how much she enjoyed having Danielle in her class. I looked at the top of Danielle's desk and there, taped to the desk, was a colored calendar with at least a dozen boxes filled with time schedules. The teacher explained that this was Danielle's special schedule. She had a reading and math class that was integrated into her day in lieu of recess and art. She explained the schedule and the various locations in the building. I asked the teacher how Danielle was supposed to know when it was time to go to her different classes and how she was supposed to find the rooms. The teacher said they tried to remind her or sometimes if the resource teacher didn't have another student she would stop by.

Well, right away I had a mental and emotional list of about ten reasons why that was unacceptable. My anger was rising along with the grip on Danielle's hand. I fought the urge that would become all too familiar, to take her away from this place. But instead in a controlled voice I asked how a six year old child is supposed to follow a complex schedule with no help. The other children were guided and escorted everywhere, but Danielle was supposed to follow a spreadsheet that requires telling time and memorizing an architectural drawing of a 12,000 square foot building. The teacher responded, "That is the way we do it."

Believe no one and nothing. They may have done it that way for three weeks, but, for Danielle, they never did it that way again. I asked for a meeting with the principal, the counselor, and the head of the school district special education department, the teachers and our private learning consultant. The accommodations they had made for Danielle looked like they were meeting their legal requirements. But when called to defend them they had to admit that Danielle wasn't receiving the agreed upon educational services. The only two people who could look me in the eye were the resource teacher and our consultant. I knew this resource teacher was someone I needed to get to know better.

Rule # 4: Mine for Gold

The resource teacher, Susan, became the first and still most outstanding teacher Danielle ever had. It is important to find the people who are devoted to children and support them. I stopped by Susan's classroom after the meeting. It was in the basement in a small, cramped space. There was a partition separating her classroom from the speech therapist. But, despite the cramped space, it was a welcoming place. Susan sat with me and told me that she really enjoyed working with Danielle. She said she had read her IEP and knew from experience that we would have a challenging road for her to learn to read. She asked me to come back as often as I could. One year after Danielle's diagnosis, three weeks into the first grade year, one congenial and one uncomfortable team meeting later, I felt a new and knowledgeable person was on our side.

Over the next few months Susan became the honest and direct translator of Danielle's brain. Susan explained to me that

Danielle could not learn to read like most children. The combination of her language disability, processing difficulties and her short term memory deficit were making it difficult for her to recognize letters or remember what she saw.

In addition to school, Danielle had a private language therapist, an occupational therapist and our learning consultant. I vowed to constantly obtain and monitor the best people in the field, but I soon realized that I could not and should not become an expert on Danielle's learning challenges. I would manage the process and find a way to pay for what she needed, but when I became too immersed in the depth of the problems I was overcome with the sheer magnitude and complexity of all she faced. I found that I could be a more positive, hopeful force if I found the best resources, understood what she needed and believed in the solutions. I could support and assist her, but my main role needed to be as her mother and not her teacher.

Be on the alert for positive experiences you and your family can share outside of school. Find something that the kids can enjoy and that will remove the focus from what can become all encompassing. Danielle was immersed in a life of specialists, but both girls were also dealing with a new school, a new house and still painful post divorce adjustments. Danielle had always had a great love for animals. Both girls were energized and happy rolling around with the dogs or riding horses when we occasionally got away to a YMCA resort an hour from our home. The girls and I would ride horses on a trail, all in a row through little streams and rocky paths. The horses were old and comatose but the girls rode until they were filthy and dropping from exhaustion. We drove home with them asking to ride some more. I decided to find a way for the girls to ride horses on the weekends. One of the best decisions I ever made.

The girls rode horses for the next ten years. Saturdays or Sundays at the barn became their salvation. They found solitude with the horses. They cleaned stalls, gave the horses baths, rode for an hour, completely focused on the physical demands. It became obvious that they both were drawing benefits from time with the horses. As they became more serious about riding and wanting to go faster and jump fences I found a teacher who gave lessons on the weekends.

But frustration soon crept in as Danielle couldn't sequence five or six directional steps to follow patterns around the ring. She also couldn't understand multiple directions. I understood her IEP well enough to know she needed to receive the information in a different way. This became one of the first of many solutions we would design together.

Danielle was five years old when she began taking horse back riding lessons and advancing in her riding skills. When we talked about how frustrating it was for her to try to learn the figure eights and follow other directions, she expressed how she heard what her teacher said and how it was all mixed up in her head. It took more than a year for us to put together strategies for her to master two courses in the ring including six turns and two low fences. There is no easy way to find these strategies; it is trial and error with dozens and dozens of each. I began to understand how frustrating her daily life must feel as we searched for ways to get information into her brain and keep it there for future use.

Ultimately we were able to devise strategies because her desire to ride and spend time with the horses was so high. When I described this to her special education teacher Susan, she explained something that would become key to her education. Susan told me that Danielle had demonstrated through this process the ability to learn in context. If she could relate to the subject matter, it seemed to provide a channel for her to learn. She could visualize the goal and the result of her work.

Learning to read was an abstract concept to Danielle. Learning to get around a riding ring and over two fences was not. We found that she could learn best if she walked the course before she tried to direct the horse around the arena. She could absorb directions by hearing them and then repeating them back in her own words to the teacher. When she would make a mistake, the teacher would touch her hand while talking with her and let Danielle try to explain why the exercise hadn't worked. That was the beginning of our understanding that her best avenue for learning was to learn in context and with a connection.

When we were told that Danielle could not understand or follow multiple directions in correct sequence I was confused because she could help bake a cake or make a sandwich. How could she know that you put the cake flour, eggs, and water into the bowl before you mix it but she couldn't follow or sequence directions? Why could she make a sandwich with several steps and not have a problem? I was convinced that if she could learn these things she could learn others.

The psychologists advised me that what I saw as a proven ability to learn was the most difficult part of Danielle's learning challenges. They described her brain as Swiss cheese. There were areas that were developed and working, but then there were large gaps where information or a task might land and there would be nothing. I took great hope from the things she had learned and mastered. While I heard what they said, I believed it was a problem in need of a solution, not a dismal prognosis which screamed limitations. They were speaking from education and experience and I was not going to listen or believe their dismal outlook.

Danielle learned to ride a horse and to lead it through a series of directions. Susan derived more and more understanding from our discussions about this frustrating, but ultimately successful process. She spent days researching and developed yet another reading strategy for Danielle. Susan constructed an elaborate program that included horses and visual cues that she used to teach Danielle to read. Susan had literally exhausted every accepted reading strategy when she designed this one for Danielle. Within a month Danielle began to retain and recognize words. Six months later we sat crunched in tiny chairs, in that cramped room where I heard Danielle read for the first time about a horse named Fred. And, for the first time, I knew in my mind what I believed in my heart, Danielle could learn. We had struck gold: Danielle, Susan and me.

Rule # 5: Fire Freely

It is essential to surround yourself with people who are positive and non judgmental. Daily life is too often shaped by the hundreds of small messages we receive, in a look or a word, which have tremendous impact on a child. You should be willing to fire people if they aren't supportive of your child's life or your family's. It is easier to fire paid therapists or even teachers than it is friends or family, but we have run the gambit. The rule is if it doesn't feel right, then it isn't right. Period.

We hired the very best people for the various therapies Danielle needed. Some people she liked and I didn't. Some I liked and she wanted nothing to do with them. It is important to realize that people who connect with children may not be as effective with adults. Choosing people your child likes, trusts and relates to is more important than choosing someone who can hold their own with an adult.

If Danielle didn't like someone I listened to her reasons. If the source of her frustration was the difficulty of the work, either in terms of content or amount, I would meet with the teacher and try to understand the work and what approach was being used. Altering the pace or the time of day of a session could sometimes resolve the problem. If a person wasn't receptive to feedback I began to look for a new person.

We are all fearful that we won't find someone better, or may end up with someone worse, but that is no excuse for inaction. And, in most cases, it is an unfounded fear. There are good people out there (Mine for Gold) but you have to keep looking to find them.

When you hire specialists, or your child has school teachers that for whatever reason don't meet her needs, you must be willing to change. Think of yourself as the customer. Would you settle for substandard food at a grocery store or a heating system in your home that didn't work? You have a choice. Your child is entitled to quantifiable quality in her education. When you ask for more, you can get more. When you request change, you can get it. But if you don't ask, you will not receive proactive people chasing after you to ask if they can do more for your child. You will most likely receive less than you need for your child.

How do you know what you need? Listen to your child. Show up at school often and request feedback. When you get people to talk with you, learn to listen. We can advocate for our children, and we should. But we are not in charge on the school's turf. Learning to listen you will find there are clues as to what is actually happening, who is in charge and where the obstacles are. If you find that your child isn't getting the one-on-one time she is supposed to receive, find out why. The source is usually in the administrative offices. So, don't crush the messenger (the teacher). Go to the boss.

There will also be friends and family who simply don't get it and some who will zap the limited energy you have available to do daily battle. Your family is entitled to the time required to give them the insight to understand what a learning disability is and to accept that your child, while learning differently, is still a very intelligent and normal child. People inadvertently (okay and some through complete ignorance and insensitivity) may say hurtful things about your child.

My policy is to provide very limited information, focus on the achievements and downplay the situation. Listening to people say such things as: "She looks normal", "Is it a birth defect", "Did you drink when you were pregnant" or "Maybe she is lazy and just needs to try harder" is hurtful, but it is frankly irrelevant in the big picture of the job you have before you. If these people have access to your child and say things that are hurtful then you should remedy that. If it is directed at you then try to let it go. You do not want to use your precious energy trying to enlighten the population about learning disabilities. Sharing information about your child is inviting people to offer their uninformed opinion. Since most people have nothing illuminating to say about what you are dealing with, the less said the better.

That brings me to you or your child's friends. When my daughter attended reading in a separate class I was concerned she would feel embarrassed by being segregated from her classmates. I was assured that since kids go to many different rooms for various reasons it would be transparent. Right.

Within a few months of entering third grade Danielle was not invited to a birthday party of a child who had been a close friend. She was very upset. Since the written party invitations were distributed at school I decided to contact the counselor to find out what was going on.

She stopped me in the hall a couple of days later to say that the friend was also very upset she couldn't invite Danielle. Apparently the child's mother felt her daughter shouldn't associate with Danielle anymore, because Danielle was in the special classroom, because something was wrong with her. I could easily be doing twenty years for murder because I wanted to harm this mother. But, I realized that this was not about Danielle. I knew we would have eventually 'fired' this family because their prejudice and ignorance would make them unacceptable to us.

Still, I hurt for Danielle. Do what you will to me, but hurt my child ...! I would like to say that was the first and only time she was treated badly by other kids and their parents, but it was not. And it never got any easier. I could be heard late at night, while holding Danielle as she cried from the rejection, saying that it was their loss (which it was). But in my heart I have never forgotten or forgiven the people who caused Danielle pain.

Bottom line: surround your family with people who are positive and supportive. There will always be friends who are only passing through your life. Family is family. If there are family members who can't or don't get it, then don't involve them in the details of your kid's life. Gloss over the details and stay global. Your home is a safe haven from a tedious world, so be selective and protective of your home, time and space.

Rule # 6: Talk Less

Many of us are accustomed to being in charge of our environment and that may extend from home to the office. Coming to grips with the fact that you are now in an environment you may know very little about can make you feel insecure, nervous and frustrated. You can be in charge of a meeting with teachers and with therapists, but you will not be helping your child. These are the people who are closest to your child's education.

Once your child has an IEP and a group of school teachers and professionals working with her, you should give everyone time to settle in to the plan. You will want to listen, observe and gather as much information as you can. If you are dissatisfied with the classroom or the schedule you should go to the source, which is usually a school counselor, special education resource or an administrator such as the principal. Ask for a meeting and let them decide who should attend. You will learn a lot about the school when you see who is included in the meeting. Share your concerns and then stop talking.

You should expect to hear the blame game: your child isn't trying, isn't completing work, and is falling short in a way that is impeding progress. Ask for specifics. Look for the clues that will help you determine how much is reasonable and how much is deflecting your attention from a possibly flawed IEP plan. The answers are most likely somewhere in between.

This type of meeting is highly complex. But your ability to learn to manage yourself in these meetings is fundamental to your child's success. Of course, you are emotionally involved because it is your child. While this is understandable, it is also counter productive. Take a step back and look at the situation. Listen to your child, listen to the school participants, gather the facts, live with them for a couple of days and then meet again.

In order to deal with facts, you will also need to get on-going information. At the beginning of each year ask for weekly progress reports. If there is work that is incomplete, milestones being missed or attitudes in need of adjustment, you will read it there.

Exhaust every possibility before you succumb to the urge to be demanding and unrelenting. Direct this measured behavior to the people who are making the decisions directly affecting your child. Just like any company, the policies and procedures are coming from the top. Go to the principal and to the school superintendent, but only after you have listened carefully, gathered your facts and prepared your case.

Rule # 7: Protect Your Privacy

The good news is that there are laws protecting your child if she has diagnosed learning disabilities. These laws are designed to allow your child the resources to have access to education creating a more level playing field with other children. The bad news is you can't access the resources without a diagnosed disability. The disability—the label—is what is required to access accommodations and to maneuver through the educational system.

While I would resist, deny, rationalize and sugar coat the label, it is a reality that clings to you like gum on the bottom of your shoe on a hot summer day. To this very day I resent that we must accept labels for our children, but I also know that it is just the beginning of a world of things we can't stand. Danielle resists the label and most often, if pressed, will refer to learning disabilities as learning differences. And she is right.

We all learn differently. We all make accommodations to help us learn or think better. Some people can't read instructions to program a computer, but if you visually show them how or tell them step by step they can do it with no problem. But, the fact remains that there is a threshold of obstacles to learning, which must be documented and addressed with what are often times complex solutions. A situation that requires a diagnosis in order to access the solutions requires a label. But, a label and a law are only the beginning of fighting the battles.

While I came to accept the label because I eventually understood that without it the school system would not act, I also knew the potential damaging ripple effect a label of any kind can have. The law provides, as does common sense, that your child's academic information is private. Be vigilant about your child's testing information and IEP. Be aware of discussions and sharing of information with teachers. Information about your child should be shared on a 'need to know basis' and is always confidential. This is non-negotiable.

Privacy in the classroom is also non-negotiable. We had too many instances where a teacher disclosed that Danielle would need to go to a certain class or have a special testing situation. That is not okay. You need to advise your child that she is entitled to absolute privacy and that if statements are made in class that violates her privacy, you need to know.

I viewed this as an issue that wasn't open to interpretation. I went directly to the teacher to inform her/him of any infraction and looked for assurance that it would never happen again. I also expected an acknowledgement (if not an apology) to Danielle. Without exception, when the teacher understood what had been said or done that caused Danielle discomfort or upset, steps were taken to correct the situation.

Rule # 8: Advocate (Don't Suffocate)

Advocating for your child is essential for her to obtain and retain the resources she will need to be successful. Your job is to know what she needs and be sure she gets access to whatever it is. However, in many cases, it is a baby steps proposition. Most Individual Education Plans (IEPs) are complex and lengthy documents. They are also detailed steps about what your child is entitled to in terms of resources and what educational goals are to be achieved. That is the beginning.

You need to be familiar with the resources agreed upon and the goals in order to be certain that they are being followed and progress is being made. You may also add additional resources outside of school to support the IEP. Having an IEP and an excellent school do not guarantee success but they are a great (and necessary) beginning.

You must advocate by being your child's eyes. What is she experiencing during the day? Is her schedule working? Are the teachers assisting her as required? When your child is young, your advocacy role is all encompassing. Everyone will be sick of you being underfoot and demanding time and attention, but that is your job. If you abdicate responsibility to the school once the IEP is developed and in place, you have in fact, surrendered. Don't do it. Stay involved. Stay present and tenacious.

Being an effective advocate also means letting your child speak for herself when she is ready and letting her falter. You may be able to say it faster and better than your child, but if you stay quiet and let her speak, you will be amazed by what you learn. And, the teachers and staff will be affected by the words and thoughts articulated by your child.

Sometimes the only way to know if the plan is working is to let it run to see if it is as good as the school specialists and educators say it is. I am not a 'trust me' person but I know that if you look at the cast of people assembled on behalf of your child and see them commit to your child's plan, then you owe them the opportunity to deliver. If they are working in concert with you and have made available the appropriate resources to help your child be successful, then the plan can be tweaked during the year. You are advocating for your child by validating that the plan is being implemented and is meeting your child's educational needs. While it may not be perfect, it needs air and time to survive. Don't suffocate the team and the plan.

However, if the plan isn't being implemented effectively you should absolutely raise your voice and demand as many meetings as it takes to get what your child needs. The fact is the squeaky wheel gets the grease. These meetings can deteriorate into adversarial situations but, even when that occurs, keep your eye on the ball. Remember your public relations mantra, "How is she doing", "Can you be specific", "Please show me her work?"

Rule # 9: Be Frustrated

Frustration is fuel for the battles we wage on behalf of our kids. Working with educators, academic bureaucrats, and legal protection is a formula for frustration. Add to the scenario that the person everyone is talking about is your child and you have an explosion waiting to happen.

Some rules to guide you:

1. Gather your facts,

2. Take twenty four hours between the upsetting situation and action,

3. Know what outcome you want for your child,

4. Get a meeting with everyone, plus a big gun (e.g. the principal or superintendent).

There will be outrageous situations that will occur. Some will be due to the complex nature of the many moving parts of an

IEP and the unique needs of your child as she travels from teacher to teacher, classroom to classroom. Some will be overt rebellion from teachers who believe they don't have to abide by the IEP. Whatever the source, the situations will occur. Be upset, be frustrated, be angry and then take action.

Give your child permission to be frustrated too. She needs to be able to express her frustration, attach a name or a situation to it and then get over it. There are many times when there are no answers and no way to fix what has occurred. Be willing to acknowledge that and attest to the fact that life isn't fair. Then put your collective energies into fighting the battles that will forward the cause. When it is a lousy situation and there is no remedy, talk it through and then let it go.

We may be resistant to anger, but it is healthy. It is also an excellent lesson for your child to be furious and express that fury as loudly and for as long as she needs to. And then to let it go and move on. It is important to hold her accountable when she is the one responsible for falling short of the plan, and it is equally important to acknowledge when we, as adults, screw up.

This is a constant emotional upheaval that lasts for years and years. Feeling sorry for yourself or allowing your child to is not okay. Of course it isn't fair. A therapist once told me that the only 'fair' is held each year in farm country where you get to eat the corn harvested right from the field and the prize winning animals are brought for display. It is what it is.

We are believers that you take the hand you are dealt and find the solutions. Note, we don't 'accept' the hand, but we do take it, analyze it and then deal with it. Danielle is a person who operates from a place of:

- What are the facts?

- What are the solutions?

- How fast can we implement them?

We both feel impatient and confused when people want to talk and talk about a problem, but, in fact, are not seeking a solution. We are about action and our energy is reserved for problems that we can resolve.

Rule # 10: Carry the Big Stick

You have to live with the label, the educational bureaucracy, and the myriad of daily frustrations. But, at the beginning and the end of each day, you have the ultimate trump card. Use it sparingly, but with absolute knowledge that you can wield the big stick. The big stick is IDEA, the law that protects your child's right to receive an education and to do so in the least restrictive environment.

Choose your battles. First evaluate the problematic situation and attempt to isolate where the breakdown is happening. Is the teacher's expectation inconsistent with the IEP? Are you confused by your child's apparent failures? Step one is to ask the teacher if she has read your child's IEP. I know that sounds obvious if not ridiculous, but you may find that the teacher has no idea about your child's learning needs or academic modifications. If the teacher is not familiar with the IEP let her know that it exists and ask for a meeting to review the plan. In elementary school it is often times much simpler to manage the IEP than the higher grade levels because there is usually one primary classroom teacher. Ask for a meeting the week before school begins. The classroom teacher, the counselor and the principal should be in attendance. The group should review the plan together and detail the learning strategies. In addition, accommodations can be made at that time. For example, if your child needs to be seated towards the front of the classroom or needs to have copies of written assignments rather than being required to copy them from the blackboard, then these should be agreed upon. This group should meet throughout the year to refine the IEP learning strategies. It is also a great idea to have a meeting at the end of the year with the teacher for the next year. Handing the baton early and familiarizing the new teacher with your child and with you will alleviate the summer stress of the unknowns regarding the next year.

If you meet resistance from the classroom teacher during the year and have tried to remedy the situation directly, then you must elevate the discussion immediately. You shouldn't assume that the counselor or principal know about problems in the classroom. Get your facts together and ask for a meeting. At this meeting you will need to detail the specific education adaptations or accommodations that are not being met. You must be prepared to show how these failures are in conflict with the IEP. The school officials know the legal protections afforded your child. Do not threaten legal action. Ask for what your child is entitled to and look for a detailed agreement and timeline for the adjustments to be made. Always remember to align your requests with the documented IEP. If you do so then the only acceptable outcome is for the changes to be made. If you don't receive agreement for the IEP to be followed then you should advise the principal that you will elevate your concerns to the superintendent and district advocates.

If you have exhausted the options available through school meetings, elevated discussions with the principal or superintendent of schools, then you have to eliminate all of the noise and bring everyone back to the reality: they are required by law to meet your child's needs. As a last resort you may need to consult with a legal representative who is versed in learning advocacy. They will be able to evaluate your individual situation and advise you. I learned that being tenacious, factual and taking small steps ultimately moved us to where we needed to be. Exhaust all possibilities through appropriate channels because the schools know that all diagnosed children carry the Big Stick and that knowledge is very motivating when they are confronted with their shortcomings. It may be unpleasant but the goal is to get the right learning environment for your child. It is tempting at times to want to be heard and to quit on the frustrating grass roots of daily school interaction, but while you may feel better (and you very well may be right about your demands) it may not benefit your child in the short or the long run. You can hold the school accountable because everyone knows they are legally accountable under IDEA. But holding them accountable in a private meeting will support ongoing, constructive communication and, in most cases, advance the ultimate goal of enhancing your child's learning environment.

Rule # 11: Celebrate Every Victory

Through all of the pain and frustration we experienced, in spite of the disappointing teachers and tiresome administrators, the overriding memories that rise above it all are the people who were there for Danielle. Teachers fell into three categories: the ones who did no harm, the ones who tormented her and me, and the ones who changed our lives. Had it not been for the extraordinary teachers, few as they were, we would have never made it through the eighteen years.

When we couldn't sink any lower or feel any worse, there would be a teacher who really "got" Danielle. A teacher who admired and respected her, a teacher who wanted her to learn and found the means to make it happen. We learned so much from these individuals and used that knowledge to develop learning strategies for other classes. We called upon these teachers to convince other teachers that developing alternative ways of teaching didn't compromise their academic standard. We understood that they were the true measure of Danielle's potential and we retold the stories of those successes over and over again.

When Danielle was in high school she had an English class that was going to be a huge challenge. There was a tremendous amount of reading and several papers. The teacher had attended the IEP meeting before school started and was clearly unhappy about being there. She said Danielle should do her best and she'd be fine. Danielle still struggled with comprehension of complex material and required strategies to recall the content. She also needed written reports to be reviewed and revised multiple times.

Danielle and I spent many, many hours each week with her dictating her thoughts while I wrote them down (her brain thinks faster than her hand writes). Sometimes the story line was out of sequence or the plot was confused and would need to be reorganized before it could be read for revisions. When she brought her draft to the teacher and asked for her comments, the teacher returned the paper with a sea of red marks and a terse note at the bottom that said Danielle needed to try harder.

We had spent six hours working on a draft, following a week of my reading the assigned book aloud to Danielle. Trying harder wasn't the solution.

I asked for a meeting with the teacher and the special education expert. The teacher was clearly angry and defensive when the meeting began. It didn't take long for her to express her displeasure at being called to this meeting and that she was doing everything necessary for Danielle. I knew the meeting was a mistake. We should have met without the special ed teacher. The situation was escalating and I knew from experience that if we didn't find a different approach the outcome would be bad.

I let a few days go by and then I stopped by to see the teacher. I expressed to her how complex and frustrating language was for Danielle but that she had proven she could master the subject matter. The high level of reading material and accompanying papers were going to require some new strategies, but we would do whatever was necessary. As I stepped back, so did she and the thaw began.

Within a week she asked Danielle to meet with her after school. They met several times a month and the teacher broke the assignments into smaller pieces. She developed note cards that highlighted the characters with key words that placed them in context for Danielle. She shared with Danielle her frustration when a student didn't try, and she shared her passion for literature which she believed wasn't measured by papers and tests.

Remarkably through the connection they formed and the strategies they developed, Danielle thrived in the class. She credited her teacher with her success but we all knew Danielle had had a real breakthrough in her education. She, at fifteen, finally saw how the connection with a teacher, the ability to develop learning strategies dependant on the course, and the proof that she could be successful in a very competitive class gave her renewed confidence.

Danielle took another more advanced English literature class with this teacher. At Danielle's final IEP meeting, this teacher patiently waited for her turn to give her feedback. When she spoke, she told us how she admired and loved Danielle for her intelligence and her determination. She spoke through tears and brought everyone else there right along with her. She said she believed that by finding the right combination to Danielle's learning we had seen her tremendous potential. She said she was grateful to Danielle and to me for not letting them fall short.

When someone cares about your child they earn a special place in your heart. When that person is a teacher, possessing knowledge and caring which result in lasting impact in your child's life, they are never forgotten. We know that the teachers who changed Danielle's life equally cherish their relationship with Danielle. We celebrate every single success. I wrote personal notes constantly to teachers to express our appreciation for their support. Whether it was an act of kindness or listening to our concerns, I let them know it made a difference.

By acknowledging the victories and all participants who share them, you demonstrate that through the good and the bad times your goal is to work with them to support your child's education. Being honorable and reasonable with both criticism and praise will go a long way towards your goal.

Rule # 12: Let Go (a little)

There will come a time when you need to begin to let go a little. You have been the advocate from the beginning and have monitored your child's education carefully. You have also felt the pain of people who judge and hurt your child. But, this happens with most children and it is something they survive. There is a natural inclination to over protect a child especially when they are dealing with the complexities of learning disabilities. But by involving your child in their own learning solutions they will be empowered more and more as they grow.

Let them go a little. This isn't to suggest you abdicate your role in their education, but do include your child in the IEP meetings when you feel it is time. The meetings take on an entirely different feeling when your child is in the room. Now teachers aren't talking 'about' her but rather 'to' her.

Let your child make decisions about homework. When your child is in middle school homework may be a nightly struggle and a huge time commitment. Danielle was willing to do her homework but she needed help. Rather than struggle about when to do homework I asked her to come up with a plan she could be comfortable with. She decided she wanted two hours after school to have a snack and relax. She would do homework before and after dinner. You should check with your child's teacher to gauge how much time your child should be spending on homework. Danielle had spelling and math homework beginning in elementary school. It took several hours to get through the homework. It was exhausting and frustrating. In talking with the teacher we found that an hour was the target amount of time for homework not three or four hours. Working with the teacher we discovered that while it might take Danielle longer to do the assigned problems, she clearly understood the content. The teacher cut her homework problems in half which allowed Danielle to master the problems but not turn every night into a homework marathon. That worked for math but spelling was an entirely different challenge. Danielle could not retrieve words and definitions at random and without some context. She would routinely fail every spelling test. This short term memory deficit and retrieval issues were documented in her testing and IEP. After several meetings with the classroom and reading teachers I began to understand why Danielle was failing the tests. She could not memorize. Danielle and I worked together to devise a way for her to remember or recognize words. The plan we proposed to her teachers was that she could match the spelling words to their definitions. We listed the words on the left and definitions on the right. Danielle would draw a line from the word to the definitions. The teachers decided that this was an acceptable accommodation and that form of testing traveled with Danielle from elementary to middle school.

Let your child struggle with the learning challenges. Let her come to terms with what she is up against because ultimately it is her challenge. And, it isn't fair, but ultimately she has to own it in order to be successful. Danielle's short term memory and language retrieval issues translate into an inability to test well. While she can qualify for extra time on tests this doesn't address the underlying problem which is that she cannot retrieve information at random. She can recall in context and she has more success when tested orally through questions and discussions, but the majority of teachers will not make that accommodation. Testing has been central to almost every battle we have fought over the years and it has never been satisfactorily resolved. Having good results on standard tests involving multiple choice or true or false questions requires short term memory at a level that Danielle does not possess. Organizing and developing complex essay questions is also a challenge. While Danielle can demonstrate her knowledge base through other testing strategies she has had to accept that without these opportunities she will have lower grades because of her testing issues. She strives to earn A's on papers, projects and in classroom participation and usually a 50% success on tests. Depending on the weight given for tests she faces a B or a C. Danielle has learned that she must always work harder at all non-testing elements of a class in order to pass. While testing accommodations do exist, they remain an area that many believe create an unfair advantage. That decision is in the hands of the school and while it may be very frustrating and perceived by the student as unfair, it is the school's prerogative. You must learn along with your child that the playing field, while intended to be made more level by learning accommodations, is in fact, not level.

Letting your child experience natural consequences is something she needs to do. In an environment where school work is a team effort it is okay to occasionally let her fly solo. It will give her insight into your role and hers. It will allow her the opportunity to carve out her level of autonomy which is ever-evolving. Giving your child the space to experiment will build her confidence and allow her to separate from you. If she chooses to go out with friends, even after you have reminded her about a project deadline, let her go. Then don't rescue her if she panics later because she ran out of time.

Danielle has learned that being totally organized is essential to managing the learning differences she lives with. She always kept a detailed planner and folders for every class assignment. She also requested a complete list of all assignments at the beginning of each school term. She found that by seeing what was required by all classes (particularly as she advanced to middle school, high school and college) she could begin assignments earlier to avoid too many projects or papers at the middle or end of a term. She also received weekly updates from every class which showed her assignments and grades to date. If she had exams condensed into one or two days she would request the exams to be rescheduled to one per day during the exam period. Danielle's organization and her initiatives described above were all her ideas to improve her ability to be successful. Letting her go allowed her to experiment and develop her own solutions.

I often told Danielle that I didn't understand a lot about what needed to be done to find learning solutions. But, I had absolute confidence in her intelligence and her ability to be successful. When Danielle fashioned a solution for a difficult teacher relationship or devised a curriculum modification with a teacher and both she and the teacher evaluated them as ultimately successful, she owned that success. Letting her go into difficult situations with confidence allowed her to chart a course built on her strengths.

Rule # 13: Be Honest

The fact is that as much as we want to defend our children we need to be honest with ourselves and with the people involved with their education. If you have issues with the school, get your facts straight and then have a conversation. Begin the conversation with an opportunity for the teacher or administrator to give his/her knowledge of the facts. Be willing to listen. Take notes and clarify the important points. If the facts don't line up then go back to your child for clarification. If the facts support that the school has fallen short then demand a remedy. If your child has fallen short then be honest with her, the school and yourself. Never shoot first and ask later. Your credibility is at stake.

When your child is in elementary school your role is by necessity very significant. Your child cannot advocate for herself or know what is right or wrong with her educational experience. Earlier we talked about staying involved and aware through day to day progress reports. Stopping by the school several times a week and being involved as a room parent gives you valuable insight into the classroom experience. As your child moves to middle school and high school you will not have the same opportunities to monitor your child's progress. You can still request the assignments and the weekly progress reports that will alert you to a problem before it becomes overwhelming or potentially jeopardizes a course grade. But the most important communication is with your child. Do sit with them when they are doing their homework. Read their projects or papers and assist where appropriate to be sure they are working to their potential. Also be open to their impressions and concerns about school.

If your child is struggling academically or is voicing concerns about a teacher listen carefully, ask questions and determine if your child needs your intervention. If they have a problem but also have a plan to address it, then let them have time to work through it. If they are upset and feel they can't manage the problem alone then begin the steps to have some meetings and discussions with the school. Ask your child what she wants to do; what she thinks would help improve the situation. Listen and respect what she says!

It is essential to get the facts straight from your child's perspective and the teacher or the school representative. Sometimes our child has either contributed to or created a problem at school. Be open to that possibility and then with the facts in hand develop a solution. When your child's special needs require constant interaction with the school it is easy to fall into a trap that makes the school the bad guy and your child the good guy. But, realistically there will be times when your child has fallen short and needs to see that she and not the teacher or school are at fault.

It is important to always get your facts straight. Parents have a natural instinct to defend their children. Being fair and informed before reacting to a situation will give you added credibility when you need it. And your child needs to know that you will be fair and vigilant when it comes to their treatment.

Rule # 14: Be Tough

We all face difficult times. Some are short lived and others are longer term. Dealing with a learning disability is a lifelong challenge. It affects all aspects of your child's life and it affects your family. Be tough, because this is a marathon. You will need to pace yourself. Be resilient, ignore the distractions and defy the odds. Being tough, while it sounds like a less than endearing trait, is actually about understanding the goal and staying the course ... no matter what.

In our case Danielle is also tough. We have managed to complement one another every step of the way. When she would hit the wall and meltdown, spewing negative forecasts of her future, I would be there to listen, to offer a hug and reiterate my belief in her. But, more times than not, the hug was also accompanied by very tough love pushing her to dig deeper, not succumb to her fears and to be strong. And, when I would finally buckle, when I reached my limit with the magnitude of the problem and the lunacy of the purported educational solutions; she would come forth with her absolute resolve. That personal balance in our relationship allowed us to keep going no matter what we encountered.

I have had hundreds of moments when all I wanted to do was take her out of the daily frustrations, keep her protected and carefree. Fortunately, I have also had thousands of tough, determined moments that kept her in the game. I always knew what was right because she always showed the guts to withstand stupidity, cruelty, and disbelievers. Our times of total defeat were private and short-lived.

I did not know as we traveled through this difficult journey that Danielle would ultimately be as resilient as she is. Her high self-esteem and tenacity have allowed her to weather adversity that many could not. The day-to-day challenges are sometimes simply too much and being prepared for that reality will provide a safe environment of understanding and acceptance for your child. There are many resources including books, websites, community, school and learning specialists who can help.

Determining what you need for your unique situation will lead you to the best resources for your family.

Danielle belonged to a group of kids at the private learning center where she went once a week for seven years (middle school through high school). Initially she participated in a group of her peers at the learning center. It was intended to allow kids with similar learning challenges to vent and to learn from others. Danielle didn't really like the peer group and dropped out after a few meetings, but four years later when she was in high school she became a group leader, with her counselor, of groups of elementary school kids who came to the learning center. She loved the groups because she had such empathy for the children and saw how fortunate she was to have support and innate strength to fight her battles. She quickly learned that many kids didn't have the same internal resources she had or the absolute belief that she has in herself.

Our children are all unique. Understanding their abilities, finding their strengths, identifying things they love, all go a long way towards maximizing their success. The balance is to allow them the opportunity to go as far as they are able but not to push them to a level of failure. That balance is a daily evolution requiring a very open mind.

Rule # 15: Suffer in Silence

I have talked about protecting your privacy and firing freely. These rules go a long way towards setting guidelines for what you share with people and deciding who spends time with your child. But this is a rule for you, parent to parent: Keep Your Own Counsel. The emotions you feel and the turmoil you experience are very real. They are also difficult for others to understand because they aren't in your shoes. People may look at you with kindness as you are unloading your feelings, but at the end of the conversation what can they truly offer you?

This is comparative to divorce. Have you ever been on the receiving end of a person telling you about their bad divorce? The horror stories, the miserable experiences that defy belief? Well, as awful as those stories can be, and as real as the pain is to the individuals involved, there is rarely anything to be gained in the recounting. People don't need to know your business. If you need to talk with someone then consider booking time with a learning specialist or a therapist. You will find a safe and private place for your thoughts and feelings.

I joined a group through our school district of parents of kids with learning disabilities. At first I thought it would be a great support system. I still remember the heart-wrenching stories as people shared their experiences, as they tried to get educational equity for their kids. The prejudices they recounted, the frustrating educators were not unfamiliar to me, but hearing their stories only made me feel horrible and hopeless. It confirmed the monumental challenge we all faced, the inequities and the hurtful situations and in only a few meetings I came to realize that, for me, there were no solutions there.

One night a father stood up and said that he had two kids; one who was gifted and one that was learning disabled. He said when he went to the parent group for the gifted kids the parents expressed resentment that tax dollars were being spent for learning disabled kids when their gifted kids didn't have nearly enough resources. He said the parents saw the money spent for learning disabled kids as a waste of money and he was furious. I figured being furious and hearing more and more sickening stories probably wasn't going to help me help Danielle.

Sharing tiny morsels of information as absolutely needed to advance your child's education is a good practice. Suffering in silence is really my dramatic way of saying we need to put our energies into managing the hand our child has been dealt. Some people may be helped by support groups or by venting with others. You should do what gives you energy and resources to cope.

You will need tremendous energy to parent and advocate for your child. How you stay healthy and centered for your child is your decision. My final word on this is to find a way to vent that follows the adage, "What happens in Vegas stays in Vegas."

Rule # 16: Let Go (a little more)

If I could have I would have fixed Danielle's learning disabilities. But, I couldn't. Nor could I protect her from all of the additional hurt she would experience because of them. My instincts as a parent were to protect Danielle and make things easier for her. But things were going to be difficult and I couldn't alter that. From the beginning I took my lead from Danielle and she taught me everything I needed to know about doing the best I could for her.

When Danielle was in middle school there were three grades, 5th, 6th and 7th with two teams in each grade. The teams all moved together to at least six different classrooms or subjects a day. If we thought that finding and dealing with one primary teacher in elementary school was a huge battle, nothing prepared us for six teachers. We set about understanding the curriculum for each class, the teaching style of the teachers, and their knowledge and willingness to follow Danielle's IEP.

It was a disaster from the first day. It was clear from the top down that the principal resented the burden and the directive of the IEP and it trickled downhill from there. We did everything possible through meetings to break down some of the barriers. We brought former teachers from the elementary school to share teaching strategies. We gave examples of successful approaches. We suggested small adaptations that might get us on a better track and, at every turn, we were met with resistance.

Add this to the middle school age and it was a very tough time. After several months it became clear that this mentality of uncooperative, combative behavior was going to continue. In one memorable hallway discussion a senior administrator suggested that putting Danielle in a private school for kids with learning disabilities might be best for everyone. In fact, there was such a school and it had an excellent reputation.

I went in search of the learning consultant who had been so valuable when we were selecting an elementary school. He had retired but his practice had evolved into a complete learning center offering a full range of services. I met with a team of people, brought them up to speed on Danielle's education so far and then shared our current frustration with the middle school. They were familiar with the school and the administration.

I asked them to meet with Danielle to ascertain if she would be better off at this special private school. They spent several hours with Danielle over the next week. When we all came together for a decision-making meeting, Danielle said something I have never forgotten. She said she wanted to stay in her current middle school and go on to public high school in our district because she wanted to go to school in the same world where she would live her life. So we set about developing a plan to make that happen. As tough as those middle school years were they contributed to Danielle's development and her absolute resolve to make it in the real world.

That was a memorable time. While my instincts may have been different than what Danielle wanted, I had faith in her ability to make that huge decision. At the same time, I feared it would be a very tough road. It was, but it was right to begin to let go.

When Danielle began to make plans for college I fully expected her to select schools close to home. She didn't. She came home with the books of colleges and began researching schools that met her selection criteria which included a program for students with learning disabilities. She insisted that an LD program would be only one of the many things she wanted in a college.

She chose two schools, one she felt pretty certain she could get into; the other was a highly competitive school. Her college counselor told her to apply to six or seven schools but she didn't. Both colleges would make their selection without disclosure of her learning disabilities. Her grades, while good, were tempered by her learning difficulties. I steeled myself against the disappointment she would feel if she wasn't accepted.

She was accepted to the college in Florida, which was her second choice. We visited there, and while it wasn't her first choice we were both excited that she definitely had a good college to attend. But, she really wanted to go to the University of Denver. She told me that they didn't go just by GPA and your ACT scores; that they made their assessment based on the entire person.

I had little faith left at that point. I had already been through the excruciating and fiercely competitive college admission process with my older daughter and was very fearful of the probable disappointment Danielle would face.

I will always remember the moment she opened her acceptance letter from University of Denver. My battered faith in educational humanity was restored in the moment when Danielle looked up at me, her big brown eyes filled with tears and a smile that conveyed the good news. When we went to visit the school I remember meeting one of the admissions counselors who said that Danielle was the kind of person they wanted, that her teacher references so impressed the committee that they knew they would be lucky to get her. As I stood next to Danielle as he spoke those words I gripped her hand and was struck again by her wisdom. She knew exactly where she wanted to go and she got there.

University of Denver is a very tough school and it was not without battles, but Danielle made it fighting every step of the way. When she hit the wall, I helped her up; and when I felt she'd had enough, she convinced me she hadn't. College is fraught with peril without the added challenges of learning disabilities, but none of the battles matter anymore because she made it through. College proved to be no more or less of a daily challenge than elementary, middle school or high school. There were some professors who didn't know or care about Danielle's learning differences and some remarkable ones who will remain forever prominent in our memories. She earned a great education and successfully added the higher level components of navigating and surviving in the real world.

Danielle has always shown me the way as she faced the challenges she came to despise. But she never felt sorry for herself or let it keep her from achieving what she wanted. An education specialist once told us that there could be no worse combination than a Type A personality with a learning disability. It certainly does seem that way on paper but that desire to achieve drives Danielle and I have always been proud to be her navigator.

Final Thoughts

Everyone who brings a new life into the world faces challenges in raising that precious child. Many times coming from a place of love and learning on the fly makes for very good parenting. And there are many unexpected challenges. Learning disabilities are invisible, but potentially life limiting if they aren't managed vigilantly. Danielle was, according to experts, incapable of learning. They were wrong. The hopes and dreams we have for our child must never be compromised. Believe in yourself, even when you are scared to death. Believe in your child and know that you can live through the battles to get to the mountain.

You can do this.

Remember the Rules:

Trust No One

No Time for Denial

Believe No One

Mine for Gold

Fire Freely

Talk Less

Protect Your Privacy

Advocate (Don't suffocate)

Be Frustrated

Carry the Big Stick

Celebrate Every Victory

Let go (a little)

Be Honest

Be Tough

Suffer in Silence

Let Go (a little more)

You will support your child to be all she can be. No one can predict what your child can achieve. When you get to the mountain know that you have really done your job well. And know that your child owns her success and will continue her climb.

About the Authors

Nancy Graves has built a successful career as a bank executive, but measures her real success in life as a parent to Danielle and Megan. She lives in the New York City area.

Danielle Graves graduated from the University of Denver in 2006. She is a Mental Health Therapist with a day treatment center in Denver. She isn't finished with her education yet, she plans to earn a doctorate degree in psychology with the ultimate goal of having a private learning consultant practice designed to work with children who have learning disabilities and their parents. Danielle still rides horses.

Nancy and Danielle are available for personal speaking engagements and we welcome the opportunity to visit with parent organizations, learning centers, teacher in-service meetings, bookstores and all interested groups either in person or via web casts. We offer inspiration on the subjects of tackling learning disabilities and successfully managing the associated life challenges.

Please contact us at www.survivinglearningdisabilities.com. We look forward to hearing from you.

978-0-595-45637-6
0-595-45637-5

www.ingramcontent.com/pod-product-compliance
Lightning Source LLC
Chambersburg PA
CBHW030413290526
45785CB00004B/1989